# HADID

Design Monographs

# HADID

ROBERT DIMERY

**Zaha Hadid** | "I don't design nice buildings," Zaha Hadid once told *The Guardian*. "I don't like them. I like architecture to have some raw, vital, earthy quality." In Hadid World, that might mean unexpected angles, or floors that become walls that become ceilings, or sinuous curves that undulate like sand dunes, or waves. She was an auteur – extraordinarily gifted, utterly committed to her vision, assuredly single-minded, a hard task master. Some critics dismissed her buildings as pretentious, their extravagance as egotistic showboating, symptomatic of the worst excesses of "starchitects" when spectacle becomes an end in its own right. But for many others, they are inspiration writ large, exhilarating spaces to fire the imagination and thrill the senses.

By the time of her death in 2016, she was not only the world's leading female architect, but part of an architectural elite that included her close friend Frank Gehry. Like Gehry, the greatest of her buildings audaciously rewrite architecture's possibilities, joyously reinventing the built environment with a love of the unexpected – jolting geometries, unlikely perspectives, organic forms. She became the first woman to win the prestigious Pritzker Prize, to pick up a RIBA Gold Medal, to win the coveted Stirling Prize (twice, in consecutive years).

But for nearly two decades, she was famous only as the architect whose buildings were never built. Whose vigorous, expressionistic submissions for design competitions – radically presented as acrylic paintings – were admired as fine art, but never attracted clients. Who once won a contest to design an opera house in Wales, only to be infamously rejected anyway – at which point lesser mortals would surely have washed their hands of architecture for good.

When Hadid came to study at London's Architectural Association in 1972, British architecture was largely a parochial affair and – much like the nation's economy – depressed and in decline. Post-war planning had attempted to meet urgent housing needs by turning to modernism: plain, unornamented

**Above.** Hadid at the opening of her first UK exhibition, at the Design Museum, London, 2007.

buildings built with the latest construction methods and contemporary materials such as concrete. High-rise, high-density living. All too often, however, the resulting buildings were cheaply built and badly maintained. Le Corbusier's vision of "cities in the skies" became detested high-rise towers whose inhabitants felt alienated and lost, deprived of a community; his "machine for living in" was breaking down. By the 1970s, chunks of post-war construction the UK's towns and cities were already being demolished.

Hadid arrived in the UK as an outsider several times over – as a woman, as an Iraqi and as someone still sympathetic to modernism. She'd seen buildings by the likes of Frank Lloyd Wright and Walter Gropius in her home city of Baghdad, where she was born in 1950. Pre-dictatorship Iraq was open to modernization and progressive ideas; women worked, some as architects. Her father co-founded the left-wing Iraqi Democratic Party, while her mother was an artist; both were forward-thinking liberals. Family trips to see ancient Sumerian cities in southern Iraq, and reed homes built by Marsh Arabs, helped spark Hadid's interest in architecture, as did the models that the architect son of one of her father's friends brought to their house. She felt equally inspired, however, by mathematics (which she went on to study at the American University in Beirut) and art.

Despite its orderly setting – a Georgian terraced house in Bedford Square, close to the British Museum in London – the Architectural Association was a vital source of experimentation and progressive ideas in those uncertain times. It employed a rolling roster of inspirational figures, including Rem Koolhaas and Elia Zenghelis, both of whom tutored her. It was through them that Hadid was introduced to Suprematism, a key modernist movement founded by Russian-Polish artist Kazimir Malevich.

In the 1920s, Malevich began producing 3D maquettes with a strongly architectural quality – rectilinear blocks of various sizes clustered together, miniature white-plaster skyscrapers. He dubbed them *arkhitektons*. Malevich was soon joined by a Russian artist working along parallel lines – El Lissitzky, whose paintings (like those of Malevich) were based on simple geometric shapes, but had an architectonic quality to them and were infused with multiple perspectives. He called them "prouns" and loosely described them as a "station where one changes from painting to architecture".

These became formative ideas for Hadid, who began to see modernism as an unfinished movement still ripe with potential, something that she could reinvestigate and take in more radical directions. She was particularly struck by Malevich's *Dissolution of a Plane* (1917), in which a tilted red rectangle appears to fade at its right-hand edge. "His geometric forms began a

**Above.** Nadja Swarovski in front of Zaha Hadid's *Malevich's Tektonik* (1976–77).

conceptual development beyond the planar, becoming forces and energies, leading to ideas about how space itself might be distorted to increase dynamism and complexity without losing continuity," she wrote in 2014. "My work explored these ideas through concepts such as explosion, fragmentation, warping and bundling. The ideas of lightness, floating and fluidity in my work all come from this research."

Realized as an acrylic painting, her fourth-year student project *Malevich's Tektonik* (1976–77) pays homage to the founder of Suprematism. Coloured *arkhitektons* are scattered around the banks of the Thames, while a fourteen-storey hotel based on Malevich's *Arkhitekton Alpha* (1920) stands on (or hangs from) the Hungerford Bridge. She graduated with the coveted Diploma Prize and briefly went on to work for Koolhaas and Zenghelis in Rotterdam at the Office for Metropolitan Architecture (OMA). But this "planet in her own inimitable orbit", in Koolhaas's words, was yearning to establish herself in her own right. In 1979, she founded Zaha Hadid Architects (ZHA), though she continued to teach at the Architectural Association throughout the following decade – while painting and drawing during the evenings.

Inspired by the dynamism of Malevich's art, Hadid began to use painting as an architectural tool, discarding the traditional tools and methods of technical representation. T squares and parallel rulers tend to dictate a certain design approach, and a two-dimensional scheme. Through painting, Hadid could create vigorous, expressive concepts that suggested 3D volume. Keenly attuned to the idea of architecture as an art form, she used her canvas to explore space and structure, just as Frank Gehry envisages his buildings as sculpture. Plenty of architects had utilized painting as part of their plans, including Frank Lloyd Wright and her former tutor Rem Koolhaas. "The use of painting overcomes a fundamental limitation of drawing: that it relies on lines, whereas built architecture is formed from surfaces," as Dr Christian McLellan and Woody Yao noted in *Zaha Hadid Architects: Evolution* (2018).

*Malevich's Tektonik* is relatively static, but Hadid soon began developing a much more dynamic style. She won her first design competition in 1983 with

**Opposite.** Zaha Hadid's *The Peak – Night, Hong Kong* (1990).

her extraordinary proposal for a five-storey luxury leisure centre called The Peak, set on a clifftop overlooking Hong Kong. Her paintings for the scheme tapped into the avant-garde explosiveness of Russian Constructivism. Views of the site are set on a diagonal and contain fragmentary forms, layering and multiple perspectives, the building visible – just about – from a wealth of different angles, by day and night. The accompanying drawings, while more straight-forward to read, had an exotic frisson of Malevich and Lissitzky about them.

Ultimately, the project was abandoned after the client lost the site. Still, Hadid's vision offered an exhilarating shot of imagination and confidence at a time when British architecture was in the doldrums. Moreover, her remarkable fine-art imagery was now creating a buzz in architectural circles. Frank Gehry was mesmerized by her paintings for The Peak, reflecting later that they "suggested a new idea, a new world, for architecture. Her style was clearly grounded in Constructivism, a movement that had inspired me for years, but Zaha's personal touch gave it a new freedom, a new engagement, a new opportunity." Patrik Schumacher saw the artworks 1983 while he was studying in Stuttgart and was inspired enough to seek out ZHA in London for an interview; he would become her closest collaborator, help facilitate the practice's crossover to using computers and is today Principal at the firm. Her profile further increased with a place at MoMA's exhibition *Deconstructivist Architecture* (1988), which also featured Gehry's work.

But although clients might admire her magnificent artworks, no one wanted to commission her to make them into buildings. They were seen as unbuildable. Many of these spectacular schemes were literally ahead of their time: it would take the advent of computer technology in the 1990s for them to become workable.

Gehry had a hand in securing Hadid her first built design, putting her forward to design a small fire station for Swiss furniture company Vitra in Weil am Rhein, Germany. Very much in the style of her paintings, the narrow building is all sharp angles and surprising perspectives – its shape dictated by conceptual lines extrapolated from the surrounding factory buildings and

**Opposite.** Vitra fire station, Weil am Rhein, 1993.

# The whole building is frozen motion, suspending the tension of alertness, ready to explode into action at any moment.
## Zaha Hadid Architects

nearby farmland – with one angular plane of reinforced concrete raised into the air like a wing. "Shafts of material colliding and forming space in a kind of edgy symphony," in Gehry's poetic summation.

With something of Gehry's sculptural heft to it, the arresting building represented a major breakthrough: the energy and vibrancy of her acrylic paintings successfully translated into physical form. She was no longer a "paper architect". Her next project, however, threatened to derail her career for good.

"To this day I am angry that this was not built," fumed Hugh Pearman – then the *Sunday Times* architecture and design critic – in 2013. "It would have been the Bilbao Guggenheim of England and Wales." The building in question was the Cardiff Bay Opera House, which would serve as a new home for Welsh National Opera and, it was hoped, become a cultural hub for local regeneration. In 1993, an international contest was launched to find an architect. Hadid won, overcoming nearly 270 competitors with what she described as her "crystal necklace", a series of glazed structures wrapped around the central auditorium; boldly angular, but not unnervingly so, and aligned neatly with the sweep of the bay, it would also create a public space. Just the injection of energy and positivity that the brief called for.

All the more bewildering, then, that she was asked to resubmit her design, along with that of rival architects including Norman Foster, for a second round – which she also won. And yet somehow, her scheme was rejected once more.

To this day, the reason why Zaha Hadid Architects lost out at Cardiff Bay remains unclear. Was her design too extreme? Certainly the tabloid press played its part, circulating rumours that funding was available either for the opera house or a new rugby ground (which became the Millennium Stadium), not both. Hugh Pearman was told by a member of the Millennium Commission, who were financing the project from National Lottery funds, that it was unbuildable ("Complete nonsense!"). Did the fact that Hadid was female and foreign-born influence the decision? Or was it simply down to resentment that a London architect, with no connections to the region, had been handed this expensive new scheme? The conservatism inherent in British architecture and politics certainly played its part, and it's no coincidence that many of the nation's more innovative architects have found a warmer reception abroad than at home.

Whatever the truth, Zaha Hadid Architects became tainted by the debacle of Cardiff Bay. It would be years before they won another competition. Hadid herself contemplated returning to teaching, or becoming a painter. Rather than fold, though, she and her practice doubled down on forging their own signature style, and working relentlessly ("I think in the 90s, honestly, none of us slept, for ten years," she told the BBC's Alan Yentob in 2013). Each new competition was an opportunity to try out new ideas, or refine old ones, expanding ZHA's palette so that when they did finally secure a new commission, they had a broad repertoire to work with.

The Landesgartenschau (1999) – initially built as a show space for a gardening festival in Weil am Rhein, home to the celebrated Vitra Fire Station – marked a modest upswing in ZHA's fortunes. The smooth integration of landscape with built environment had been a feature of Hadid's designs since at least The Peak. Here, she ran a series of paths through, around and over a central pavilion – housing a café, exhibition hall and today an environmental centre – which followed the contours of the surrounding terrain so closely that it appeared to emerge from and dip back into it. Slender and low-rise, it takes its lead from the natural world where, in contrast to the urban environment, transitions between types of habitat are fluid and nuanced.

Hadid triumphantly made up any lost ground with Cincinnati's Lois and Richard Rosenthal Center for Contemporary Art (2003), which made her the first female architect to design a major modern art gallery in the USA. "The most important American building to be completed since the Cold War,"

**Above.** Landscape Formation One (LFOne), Weil am Rhein, 1999.

declared *The New York Times*. The exterior is defined by block-like expanses of concrete in white and black, not unlike a Malevichian *arkhitekton*; at street level, the pavement continues into the foyer, then audaciously continues up a wall to the ceiling, an "urban carpet" (Hadid's term) to draw in passers-by who might not otherwise wander in. Its restricted site, on a street corner in Cincinnati, also meant that it had to be built as a vertical museum – a first for Hadid, whose previous projects had all been low-lying – which inspired a series of brilliant, space-maximizing design initiatives, including interlocking, or "nesting", galleries. The narrow zig-zagging flights of stairs don't align, allowing visitors glimpses into galleries as they pass. It's intended to invite browsing, which creates the possibility of unexpected and exciting discoveries.

Completed while the Rosenthal Center was still being built, Hadid's elegant Bergisel Ski Jump (2002) in Innsbruck, Austria, has the kind of sleek curves that would become her trademark. Rising some 50 metres (164 feet) into the air, its modernistically pared-down profile is topped with a viewing gallery and café, offering panoramic views out to Innsbruck and its surroundings, from which the ski ramp descends gracefully, echoing the slope of the Bergisel mountain on which it stands.

Successful designs often have an afterlife. The ski jump's slightly staggered verticality would later inspire the only private home that Hadid completed during her lifetime, the four-storey Capital Hill Residence (2018) in Moscow whose apex, like that of the ski jump, looks out over treetops. "It is, in the words of both architect and client, a 'dream house'," enthused the *Financial Times*, "as much fantasy as reality, an idea of architecture that still seems somehow impossible" – a description that could apply to so many of Hadid's projects.

Nearly ten years after the Cardiff Bay debacle, Zaha Hadid finally received the ultimate accolade. In 2004, in recognition of inspirational works such as the Vitra Fire Station and Rosenthal Center, she became the first female architect to be awarded the coveted Pritzker Prize.

The Rosenthal Center was the first ZHA project to employ computer-aided design (CAD), something that Frank Gehry was investigating in parallel. "I

**Opposite.** Bergisel Ski Jump, Innsbruck, 2002.

**Above.** Rosenthal Center for Contemporary Art, Cincinnati, 2003.

tried to find a way to use the clarity of those machines to keep the architect in the role of master builder, as the leader of the team directing the construction from the beginning to the end," he recalled later, "rather than ceding control to a team of engineers and technical experts." CAD had emerged in the 1960s, but it wasn't picked up by architects until thirty years later, in tandem with ZHA's professional coming of age.

As a passionate and versatile artist of the analogue world, Hadid was initially reluctant to embrace digital technology. But she overcame her reservations once she understood its potential for generating complex geometric curves and adding a sinuous flow to building designs. Driven in particular by Patrik Schumacher, Zaha Hadid Architects would later become pioneers in "parametricism" (a term he coined): data is fed into a computer, which then suggests complex forms that an architect would be unlikely to come up with alone. Change one point in the scheme and the rest of it alters to reflect the amendment. As parametric curves are generated mathematically, it's possible to programme code to influence the algorithms and, therefore, the shapes they produce. Hadid frequently sought inspiration from nature; now, via CAD, she could mirror its complexities more closely and generate more organic, less predictable forms.

What's more, computers were no longer limited simply to visualizing a design that an architect had worked up. Provided with key data, they could autonomously produce their own designs, effectively adding their own contributions to a scheme that could then be taken up and further refined by designers, adding another level of malleability to the process. Drawings and sketches could also be inputted, then modified ad infinitum.

All that notwithstanding, for some time now architects and designers have been aware that some software programs tend to gravitate towards specific styles, repeatedly generating designs with common features. Hadid also observed that CAD had a tendency to produce isolated (albeit spectacular) buildings that ignored the context of their environment, a criticism that was to be levelled at some ZHA projects in years to come.

CAD would revolutionize ZHA's working practice. Previously, as was architectural convention, team members worked up 3D models of buildings, often in paper or highly polished resin. But eventually, model-making by hand would be phased out altogether – highly unusual for an architecture firm. Models can be created far more rapidly with 3D printing, though these are used for checks and verifications during development, rather than as part of the initial design process.

Technology had finally caught up with her. And it wouldn't be long before clients did too. In one year, ZHA was commissioned to produce three of its most distinctive works: the Bergisel Ski Jump, the Phaeno Science Centre in Wolfsburg, Germany (2005), and Rome's National Museum of Arts of the Twenty-first Century (2010). Better known as MAXXI, it was – remarkably – the first museum for contemporary art, architecture and design in the Italian capital, and represented a marked evolution in Hadid's style.

MAXXI's footprint is constricted by neighbouring buildings, including military barracks. However, ZHA worked within those constraints to produce an intriguing structure that, seen from above, is criss-crossed with serpentine oblong tubes that initially seem most like a junction of train tracks but are actually steel fins within the roof structure. Dominating the front, Gallery Five's angled window casts an eye on to the city.

The building's smooth concrete walls cross over and bifurcate, creating an aesthetically intriguing effect, but also reinforcing structural stability – an essential feature as the region is susceptible to earthquakes. Hadid referred to them as "a delta of rivers but they are frozen in time". Beneath the concrete behemoth lies a courtyard and public space, a feature that was to recur in her celebrated Phaeno Science Centre.

Step inside, and you're greeted by a melange of steel staircases and bridges in black and white – an open invitation to wander around – that runs through the whole building. Some observers found the layout confusing, but it was utterly in keeping with Hadid's belief in encouraging visitors to browse, to be surprised and intrigued. In a description that would have delighted Hadid, Rowan Moore wrote, "It is something you can't comprehend in one go, that has to be unravelled through walking around and into it."

With its unpredictable form, off-kilter walls and fluid spaces, MAXXI represented key aspects of what was to become Zaha Hadid's signature style. You don't need corners or straight lines to guide you when you're walking in a landscape, as she often reminded people. "The world is not a rectangle," she once mused to *The Guardian*. "You don't go into a park and say: 'My God, we don't have any corners.'" If you're not spoon-fed directions, who knows what you might discover? Like many of her finest buildings, MAXXI gives the impression of constant motion, a building transforming as you pass through it. In a 2013 BBC One *Imagine* documentary on Hadid, Hugh Pearman talks of imagining its tendrils spreading out into the rest of the city, as if it can't be contained.

**Opposite.** MAXXI, Rome, 2009.

**Above.** Interior of MAXXI, Rome, 2009.

# You're not necessarily lost, but you don't know exactly where you are.
Zaha Hadid, BBC Radio 3
*Sunday Feature*, 2010

There's something almost operatic about MAXXI's vast, dramatic spaces. It isn't simply a building for displaying art; it's an artwork in itself, as worthy of attention as any of its exhibits. The works that would represent the museum's collection hadn't yet been purchased, so there was no requirement to design to fit them; ZHA had carte blanche to indulge themselves.

Or overindulge? Some critics argued that the architecture overshadows the collection, that the architect's ego had won out. And anyway, how could you display art on walls that weren't straight? Then again, Frank Lloyd Wright's curvaceous Guggenheim Museum (1959) in New York faced the same criticism. And that's done all right for itself.

Perhaps it is best to think of MAXXI as a shot of twenty-first-century neo-baroque to complement Rome's baroque splendours, a reviving burst of energy and spirit for an ancient city. And, more prosaically, an attempt to recreate the Gehry "Bilbao effect" on the banks of the Tiber. Hadid's projects frequently have the happy knack of boosting local economies. RIBA had no doubts, anyway. In 2010, MAXXI won Zaha Hadid the Stirling Prize, the first time it had ever been awarded to a woman.

While MAXXI was still under construction, Hadid won and completed two commissions in Germany. Both provided further evidence of her growing confidence and ability as an architect. For BMW's site on the outskirts of Leipzig, she crafted a building set at the heart of the firm's complex of buildings, and through which snakes a car assembly line. Watching an incomplete chassis move along it between production units acts as a reminder that at the heart of all those administrative tasks is the production of a world-famous brand. The huge, staggered floors allow views across the whole building from any point.

The enormous Phaeno Science Centre (2005) in Wolfsburg was envisaged as a "magic box", something to arouse curiosity in its visitors and encourage them to explore. Standing in the atrium, visitors are given enticing glimpses into the museum's different levels. ("In our architecture, with every step new vistas open and close," Patrik Schumacher told the BBC in 2013. He also referred to the "information richness" of ZHA's buildings.) Structurally, it sits on cone-shaped concrete stilts that are large enough to accommodate not only a shop, café and restaurant but a theatre and laboratory too. The expansive exhibition hall offers a wealth of angles and odd perspectives. Phaeno's flanks and underbelly are flecked with windows set diagonally, while a public plaza lies below. The building also serves to symbolically unite two discrete halves of the city, placed midway between a massive Volkswagen plant and a residential area.

In her Pritzker Prize acceptance speech, Hadid noted, "The new digital design tools pull architecture into an uncharted territory of opportunity. This is one of my current preoccupations: the development of an organic language of architecture, based on these new tools, which allow us to integrate highly complex forms into a fluid and seamless whole."

Certainly, this building embraced adventurous curved lines more comprehensively than previous projects, something that had become possible through parametric design. But in some respects, technology was still struggling to catch up with Hadid's vision. In 2013, structural engineer Professor Hanif Kara reminisced, "It took us nearly eighteen months to get computers to a level [...] to push the software as we were designing the building to a level where we could actually understand the gravitational forces." He revealed that it took him around two years to confess to Hadid that they couldn't even draw up the design for the Phaeno Science Centre, let alone make it.

Unlike many of her peers – and, for that matter, some of the more recent projects under the ZHA imprint – such buildings work at a human scale. And provide a welcome respite from phallocentric architecture, too.

Broadly speaking, her building for BMW exhibits Hadid's early preference for jagged forms. The style continued with her Spittelau Viaducts (2005) housing project in Vienna, Austria, whose four white riverside buildings lean at playful angles around a disused railway viaduct. The same angled forms reappeared at Maggie's Centre Fife (2006), part of a national network of

resource and counselling centres for people with cancer. Her first UK commission, designed free of charge, this single-storey construction is a dynamically angular affair, its metal roof slanting down to ground level and across the entrance like an origami fold, its profile picking up on the surrounding treeline.

**Above.** Phaeno Science Centre, Wolfsburg, 2005.

In the context of the grand statement buildings she has created, it makes for a refreshing contrast to see a master architect working on a smaller scale. Witness also her extension for Copenhagen's Ordrupgaard Museum (2005), subtly cast in black concrete that alters its shades according to the light and weather conditions. It sits on a grassy slope in the museum's gardens, whose topography influenced the design's gentle undulations (its profile has earned it the affectionate nickname of "beached whale"). Expansive glass windows cover the sides, reflecting nearby trees and allowing the building to blend into its location, while light slits in the roof help visitors to orientate themselves. In a feature that recurs in Hadid's designs, the walls, floor and ceiling are one.

Her scheme for four stations along Innsbruck's Nordpark funicular railway (2007) incorporated shell-like awnings to cover entrances and exits – concrete substructures covered in melted glass, they seemed to float atop concrete plinths. Project architect Thomas Vietzke and his team employed software to generate the fluid forms, which he describes as "like a piece of melting ice sitting in the landscape like a piece of glacier". It was entirely fitting for its location, while also anticipating her later work for the Serpentine Sackler Gallery in London's Hyde Park.

At the same time, ZHA was working on two bridges. Completed the year after her Nordpark stations, the Bridge Pavilion (2008) in Zaragoza, Spain, was built as a gateway for an international exposition held in the city that year. It not only connects the two sides of the Ebro river, but also incorporates exhibition halls along the way. The Sheikh Zayed Bridge (2010), a new third crossing connecting Abu Dhabi island with the southern shore of the Persian Gulf, was on an altogether larger scale, with a pair of four-lane carriageways bestride by an asymmetrical triumvirate of steel arches that were styled after sand dunes.

Despite her burgeoning international profile, Hadid had long remained the proverbial prophet without honour in her own country – although a CBE in 2002 and damehood in 2012 redressed some of the balance. Still, very few of her designs were built in the United Kingdom; ZHA has a greater presence in

**Opposite.** Ordrupgaard Museum extension, Copenhagen, 2005.

**Above.** Evelyn Grace Academy, London, 2010.

the Middle and Far East. She confessed that she only truly felt acknowledged in the UK when she was awarded her second Stirling Prize in 2011 for the Evelyn Grace Academy (2010) in Brixton, London, which beat that year's favourite, the velodrome for the London 2012 Olympic Games. Housing four smaller "schools-within-schools", the school's main building is Z-shaped, a motif picked up in the glass and steel frontages, but is also characterized by Hadid's trademark angles and curves. It boasts large recreation areas and an expansive dining and sports hall, although its prime talking point was a running track that dramatically passed under a bridge on the site, dividing its main building into two. That the academy had to be squeezed into restricted space between two busy roads made the design all the more impressive.

With the Guangzhou Opera House (2010), intended to boost the cultural heft of a major financial hub in China, Hadid produced one of the earliest examples of a building envisaged as an overall topography. The main 1,800-seater

**If someone asks me to do a library I wouldn't say I don't want to do it because of where it is. It's important to engage with these countries because it connects them to the rest of the world.**
Zaha Hadid, *The Guardian*, 2013

Architects are now being called out on issues that didn't trouble previous generations – everything from working for contentious regimes to the environmental impact of their constructions. Like many of her peers, Hadid was frequently asked why she didn't at least use her considerable profile to raise concerns over problematic clients in interviews.

In 2012, she received further recognition in the form of the Jane Drew Prize for Architecture. Alongside the fact of her extraordinary designs, her bloody-minded persistence and determination to succeed in the face of misogyny were certainly at the forefront of the jury's minds when they acknowledged "her outstanding contribution to the status of women in architecture". But ArchDaily's Vanessa Quirk raised the thought-provoking point that Drew – who was, among other things, the first woman elected to RIBA's council and the Architectural Association's first female president – believed in "a moral rather than a purely materialistic view of Architecture"; for Quirk, Hadid's priority was simply to create "High Art".

From the turn of the millennium, and in tandem with many other leading architects, ZHA began to expand the brand. Formed in 2006, Zaha Hadid Design (ZHD) develops projects for fashion, furnishings and everything that falls under the umbrella of "product design"; it has worked on Adidas trainers with Pharrell Williams and perfume bottles for Donna Karan.

Parametricism had become an indispensable part of the ZHA toolbox, and naturally crossed over into ZHD's portfolio too. Take her Z-Scape lounge furniture (2000–present), eleven fragment-like pieces that can be reconfigured and which derive their intriguingly amorphous lines from the geology of glaciers. Or the Zephyr sofa (2013), inspired by the forms that erosion sculpts out of rock. Or the petal-like Flow vase (2006–07), part vessel, part sculpture. For David Gill Gallery, ZHA devised the Liquid Glacial furniture range, which looks like water arrested in mid-flow, while the silvery surfaces of the Loa and Vesu vases (2014) for Wiener Silber ripple beguilingly. She even designed a statuette for the Brit Awards. Unveiled posthumously in December 2016, her curvaceous Britannia design was seen through to completion by ZHD's Maha Kutay.

With her extravagant personality, Hadid also made a natural fit as a stage set designer. She provided the backdrops for the Pet Shop Boys' 1999–2000 *Nightlife* tour, winning acclaim for a modular set that could change as the performance progressed. ("You could see them as stage sets, particularly for a rock show, because they're very dynamic," singer Neil Tennant observed. "I can just imagine standing on the edge of one with the wind machine on and a big coat fluttering in the breeze.") She also developed the Mind Zone exhibit at the Millennium Dome – three discrete spaces exploring mental input, process and output, whose walls, floors and ceilings unfolded from one continuous surface.

The serpentine forms and sensual lines of standout buildings such as the Heydar Aliyev Cultural Centre earned Hadid the sobriquet "Queen of the Curve", but in the last few years of her life she consistently demonstrated the breadth and versatility of her palette. Pierres Vives (2012), a municipal building in Montpellier, France, houses three separate facilities. Based on the concept of a tree of knowledge, the layout branches out from a public archive to connect to a *médiathèque* and sports department housed elsewhere in the building. Its concrete exterior is run through with recessed, green-tinted windows (marking out public spaces and hallways) set in bifurcating channels.

No less striking is the Eli and Edythe Broad Art Museum (2012) on the campus of Michigan State University, USA. Fittingly for a museum for modern art, its dynamic exterior comprises façades of pleated steel and glass set at fantastic angles, altering in hue as the daylight changes. (Behind the vertical pleats are interior staircases.) No idle architectural fancy, the playful angles of the frontage tie in with pathways and sightlines in the surrounding environment, while the offset walls and bridges within pick up on the diagonal theme, making for a thrillingly diverse set of perspectives. As one might expect, the internal spaces are vast.

Two London commissions reflected the ongoing diversity of ZHA's work. The Serpentine North Gallery (2013; formerly known as the Sackler Gallery) was created by extending an underused storage area in what had once been a gunpowder store, the Magazine. Hadid's intervention added some 900 square metres (9,690 square feet) to the Serpentine's footprint in the form of a new, warmly received exhibition space. The main talking point, however, was the accompanying glass-walled restaurant covered by a swooping tensile PTFE-coated glass fibre roof, which touches the ground at three points like drooping flower petals, and which emerges within from five stem-like steel columns, each opening to the sky at their apex, allowing light

**Above.** Flow vase for Serralunga, 2007.

**Above.** "Mathematics: The Winton Gallery" at the London Science Museum, 2016.

to filter down. The roof was ZHA's first permanent tensile construction and intended, as they saw it, "to complement the calm and solid classical building with a light, transparent, dynamic and distinctly contemporary space of the twenty-first century".

Not everyone was convinced: *The Telegraph* found it "aggressive and banal", while *The Guardian* compared it to "a wedding marquee battling with a stiff breeze" and carped, "It is not quite clear what function all this overwrought writhing serves." The barb chimes with a criticism that ZHA has faced increasingly over the years: possibly owing to the dominance of

CAD in their design process, they tend to produce buildings whose extravagance is an end in itself.

The same could be said of many of Hadid's contemporaries, of course. With the increasing sophistication of design software, and the technical advances made by engineering firms, the only practical constraints to a building scheme mostly come down to structural limitations or those related to the materials used. Given which, the onus is on architects to be self-disciplined enough not to allow their projects to teeter over into overindulgence.

No such brickbats for the Science Museum's Winton Gallery (2016), which thrillingly reimagined an existing exhibition room devoted to mathematics. Its centrepiece is a suspended Handley Page "Gugnunc" biplane, an experimental vehicle designed in 1929. It became the starting point for the startling design: the voluptuous folds and curves surrounding the aircraft, and indeed the entire ground layout of the space, from displays to seating, are based on simulated airflow fields. Intelligently devised and aesthetically engaging, the new gallery – which picked up RIBA's London Award – demonstrates one way that mathematics influences technology and, as a result, our environment. Happily, it also prompted an upsurge in visitor numbers.

Poignantly, the Winton Gallery was to become the first of Hadid's projects to be completed posthumously. It opened in December 2016, nine months after she died from a heart attack in Miami, having initially been hospitalized with bronchitis. She was only sixty-five.

With the long lead times inherent in architecture, many projects that Hadid contributed to only saw the light of day after her passing, among them ZHA's first high-rises. At their best, they marry technological excellence to imaginative spark.

Take the RIBA Award-winning Jockey Club Innovation Tower (2014) in Hong Kong, a fifteen-storey building set on a narrow plot and which houses two design institutions. Labs, workshops, exhibition spaces, classrooms and studios are housed in a tower shaped like an off-kilter mountainside; its striated levels appear like geological layers.

Or Wangjing SOHO (2014) north-east of Beijing in China, a mixed-use complex of three interlinked edifices with the roundness of pebbles but an elevation approaching that of mountains – the tallest tops out at 200 metres

# As a woman in architecture, you're always an outsider. It's okay, I like being on the edge.
Zaha Hadid, *Financial Times*, 2015

(656 feet). Strips of white aluminium louvres cling to the sides to help moderate sunlight. Set in a tech hotspot, and incorporating a host of open-plan offices, it's accompanied by a 60,000-square metre (645,830-square foot) park. The structure was to generate widespread comment, and not just because of its architecture. Computer design has revolutionized architecture, but computers rely on data, and data can be copied. Even as the buildings were being constructed, a remarkably similar complex – Meiquan 22nd Century – was springing up in Chongqing, a city in the south-west of the country. No intellectual property rights existed in Asia to guard against copying, or closely imitating, another architect's plans.

Far and Middle Eastern countries with deep pockets and an openness to architectural showmanship have given ZHA's more fantastical designs a warm welcome, with increasingly jaw-dropping constructions popping up over the past decade or so. Beijing's Galaxy SOHO (2012) comprises four interconnecting ovoid buildings whose exteriors were partly inspired by terraced rice fields. Leeza SOHO (2019) – also in the Chinese capital and one of the last buildings that benefited from Hadid's direct input – features what may be the tallest atrium in the world, twisting upwards for 194 metres (636 feet). Linked by a quartet of skybridges, the skyscraper's two towers rotate at forty-five degrees to each other in what ZHA rather fancifully describes as a "dynamic pas de deux". Reportedly inspired by Chinese jade carving, the forty-storey Morpheus Hotel (2018) – a self-described "ultra-luxury" hotel at City of Dreams resort, Cotai, Macau – has a frontage that contorts inwards, encased in a latticework exoskeleton.

What unites them all, and links them to the Opus Hotel (2020) in Dubai, UAE, is the use of voids that interrupt the architecture, enabling light to

**Above.** Morpheus Hotel, Macau, 2018.

penetrate the interiors from all sides and also offering views through to cityscapes on the other side. Leeza SOHO's atrium is the most conventional of the lot. But three asymmetrical holes punctuate Morpheus's façades like bullet holes, while Galaxy SOHO has both internal and external atria with diverse configurations, ground-level spaces inspired by traditional Chinese courtyards and a central "canyon". Looking at Morpheus or Opus (whose eight-storey gap was inspired by the idea of a dissolving ice cube), it's difficult to say where architecture ends and sculpture starts; they have something of Salvador Dalí's melting clocks about them.

A different sort of surrealism distinguishes the Havenhuis, or Port Authority Building (2016) in Antwerp, Belgium. An existing fire station was redeveloped to accommodate 500 workers from around the port in a new headquarters, spectacularly topped by a new extension that appears to float above the restored building, though it takes concrete pillars and hundreds of tonnes of steel support it; a bridge connects the two. The extension's glazed windows combine opaque and transparent glazing set at various angles, and create an effect reminiscent of a jewel's facets (a nod there to Antwerp's role as the global hub of the diamond trade). The overall structure, however, more closely resembles a ship's prow pointing towards the Scheldt, the river on which Antwerp was founded.

Such outside-the-box vision had long distinguished Hadid's portfolio, and was reflected in her being awarded the RIBA Gold Medal – she was the first ever solo female recipient – just a month before her passing. "We now see more established female architects all the time," she stated in her acceptance speech, adding a cautionary, "That doesn't mean it's easy."

True enough. In a thoughtful obituary, Frank Gehry observed that although around half the architecture graduates in the USA were female, far fewer worked as practising architects, and fewer still in senior roles. (In 2017, the University of Pennsylvania School of Design claimed that just 22 per cent of all licensed architects in the USA were women, with 17 per cent working as partners or principals.) "Zaha was the exception, and she became a model," Gehry noted. But was she the exception that proves the rule? Gender pay gaps in architecture have actually widened, while issues such as bullying and discrimination (including a reluctance to employ female architects who may then take time out to have a family) remain depressingly present. Architecture remains something of a boys' club and no female architect before or since has achieved Hadid's global status. Perhaps it's no coincidence that she remained singularly committed to her career, never stepping back for relationships or motherhood.

In comparison with ZHA's double-take buildings in China and the UAE, 520 West 28th (2017), a prestigious eleven-storey condominium overlooking New York's High Line park, might seem relatively tame. But it ranks among the city's finest towers, not least for its signature interlocking steel chevrons that wrap around the building, extending at the sides to become balconies and canopies, and flag up the design of the split-level apartments within. The building wasn't a ZHA production, though, as the firm weren't licensed to practise in New York; Hadid's contribution was as a lead designer, as part of a team alongside her closest and longest-serving collaborator, Patrik Schumacher.

Three years after her death, the largest project Hadid was ever involved with came to fruition. Beijing Daxing International Airport (2019) was a mere five years in the making. It has the profile of a starfish from above, though Hadid herself envisaged it as a phoenix in flight. The six "arms" cover some 700,000 square metres (7,534,740 square feet) – or around twice the size of Heathrow Airport's Terminal 5 – making it the largest single-building terminal in the world.

An estimated 100 million passengers will be passing through annually by 2040. What will they find? A sleek aero-palace bedecked in parabolic arcs with long curvilinear lines, some on the ceiling, to help guide travellers through the cavernous space. It's topped off with 350,000-square metre (3,767,369-square foot) steel hyperboloid roof. Daylight pours down from huge, latticed skylights, via eight tulip-shaped funnels that also support the roof, onto highly polished white floors. The terminal's six arms meet at a central hub, where the ceiling tops out at a height of 45 metres (148 feet). Thanks to the radial design, to walk from the most distant gate to the heart of the building takes only around eight minutes. All in all, a spectacular statement piece and one, so far, that has been warmly received by users and critics alike.

Like any individual who challenges and then changes the fabric of their field, Zaha Hadid had her share of missteps. She elicited howls of protest –

from journalists critical of the controversial clients she sometimes courted, to exasperated clients as they watched their budgets sailing skywards and out of sight. Sometimes her buildings clearly take their lead from a site's topography or cultural traditions; at other times, they seem to exist in a space and time of their own, in proud isolation. For good or ill, and like Hadid herself, they don't compromise.

Commentators were as drawn to Hadid's sartorial flamboyance as her architecture. She once revealed that she loved Japanese designers such as Issey Miyake and Yohji Yamamoto "because their clothes are often asymmetrical and quite theatrical" – not unlike her buildings, then. She was dubbed a diva, but as she famously pointed out, a male architect wouldn't have attracted that epithet. And that tag casually overlooks the years of dedicated graft she put in in the face of repeated rejection, her galvanizing impatience with architectural conventions and a steely belief in the worth of her ideas.

Her most remarkable buildings have something of a magic trick about them. They beguile us, make us want to look again to see how the illusion has been achieved. Above all, and in common with all pioneers in her field, they ask you to reimagine what architecture can be. "Without ever building," observed Rolf Fehlbaum – the Vitra chairman for whom she once built a fire station – "Zaha Hadid would have radically expanded architecture's repertoire of spatial articulation." Or as Hadid herself neatly summed up: "There are 360 degrees, so why stick to one?"

**Opposite.** 520 West 28th, New York, 2017.
**Overleaf.** Guangzhou Opera House, Guangzhou, 2010.

[01, 02] Vitra fire station, Weil am Rhein, 1993. [03, 04] Rosenthal Center for Contemporary Art, Cincinnati, 2003. [05] Nordpark Railway station, Innsbruck, 2007.

[06] BMW Central Building, Leipzig, 2005. [07, 08] Ordrupgaard Museum extension, Copenhagen, 2005. [09] Phaeno Science Centre, Wolfsburg, 2005. [10] Spittelau Viaducts Housing, Vienna, 2006. [11] Maggie's Cancer Centre, Fife, 2006.

[12] Pavilion Bridge, Zaragoza, 2008. [13] Sheikh Zayed Bridge, Abu Dhabi, 2010.

[14] CMA CGM Headquarters, Marseille, 2010. [15] Riverside Museum of Transport, Glasgow, 2011. [16] Eli and Edythe Broad Art Musuem, East Lansing, 2012. [17] Galaxy SOHO, Beijing, 2012.

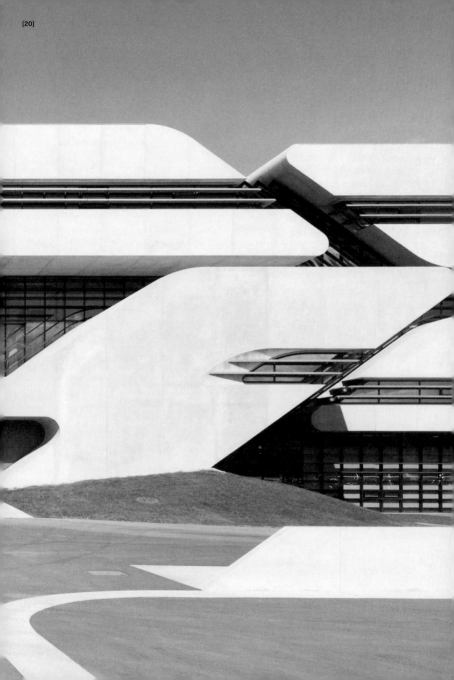

[18, 19] London Aquatics Centre, London, 2011. [20, 21] Pierres Vives Archive and Library, Montpellier, 2012. [22, 23] Dongdaemun Design Plaza, Seoul, 2014.

## 27

[24] Heydar Aliyev Cultural Centre, Baku, 2012. [25, 26] Serpentine North Gallery, London, 2013. [27] Library and Learning Centre, University of Economics, Vienna, 2013.

[28, 29] Jockey Club Innovation Tower, Hong Kong, 2014. [30] Wangjing SOHO, Beijing, 2014. [31] Nanjing Hotel and International Youth Cultural Centre, Nanjing, 2018.

[31]

[32] Port Authority Building, Antwerp, 2016. [33] Maritime Terminal, Salerno, 2016.
[34] Generali Tower, Milan, 2018.

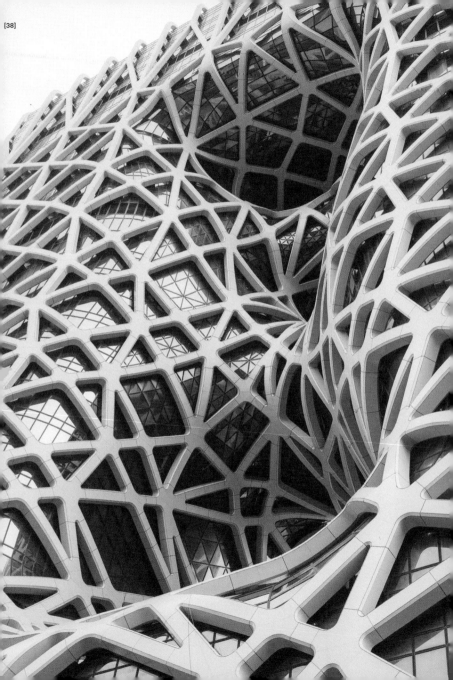

[35] Leeza SOHO, Beijing, 2019. [36] Afragola train station, Naples, 2017. [37, 38] Morpheus Hotel, Macau, 2018. [39] Opus Hotel, Dubai, 2020.

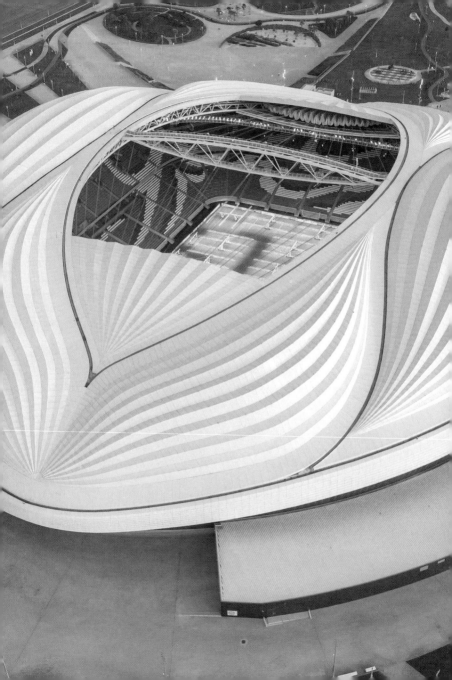

[40, 41] Daxing International Airport, Beijing, 2019. [42, 43] Al Janoub Stadium, Al Wakrah, 2019. [44] Grand Theatre of Rabat, Rabat, 2023. [45] Sky Park, Bratislava, scheduled 2025.

[47]

[48]

[46] Moraine sofa for Sawaya & Moroni, 2000. [47] Z.Car, 2007. [48] Moon System sofa for B&B Italia, 2007. [49] Mew table for Sawaya & Moroni, 2015. [50] VorteXX chandelier, with Patrik Schumacher, for Sawaya & Moroni in collaboration with Zumtobel, 2005.

[51] Aria suspension light for Slamp, 2013. [52] NOVA shoe for United Nude, 2013.
[53] Zephyr sofa (foreground) at the Fudge pop-up salon, for Cassina, 2013.

[54] Liquid Glacial chair for David Gill Gallery, 2015. [55] UltraStellar double-seat bench for David Gill Gallery, 2016.

The publishers would like to thank the following sources for their kind permission to reproduce the pictures in this book.

**Alamy** /Abaca Press 97/Andrew Benton 83/Arcaid Images 28, 48, 49/B.O'Kane 22/Bildarchiv Monheim GmbH 25, 52–3/chuck 95/Chris Gascoigne-VIEW 59/dpa picture alliance 108/Edmund Sumner-VIEW 27/ Hemis 60–61/Hufton+Crow-VIEW 31, 74–5/Iain Masterton 80/ imageBROKER.com GmbH & Co. KG 64/Marcus Peel-VIEW 100t, 106–7/ Michal Sikorski 15, 46, 47/Nathan Willock-VIEW 101b, 103/Paul Riddle-VIEW 70/Peter Chisholm 65/Peter Jordan_EU 50–1/Petr Svarc 58/Serhii Chrucky 18/Tuimages 39, 91/ukartpics 09/Vito Di Stefano 96. **Bridgeman** / Andrea Jemolo 21/Paul Riddle/View/Artedia 68/San Francisco Museum of Modern Art 10, 109. **Getty Images** /Bloomberg 07/CARLO HERMANN 86/ Jessica Hromas 105/Kennyzheng 90/NIKLAS HALLE'N 36/Tim Graham 55/ View Pictures 42, 54, 67, 69, 70, 89, 101t. © **Sawaya & Moroni, Milan, Italy www.sawayamoroni.com** 100, 102. **Serralunga** 35. **Shutterstock** / ABCDStock 04–5/jksz.photography 72/Joshua Davenport 73/KILOVISION 94/lauravr 13/Marin04ka 78–9/martin.dlugo 99/Martine314 84–85/MC MEDIASTUDIO 87/meunierd 16/Mounir Taha 98/Nattakit Jeerapatmaitree 92–93/Pani Garmyder 56–7/Pol.Albarran 110/Ron Ellis 76, 77/Sinseeho 81/ solkafa 62–63/SNEHIT PHOTO 66/testing 88/Wait for Light 82. © **Slamp/ Thomas Pagani** 104. **Unsplash** /Abdelmalek Bensetti 30/Scarbor Siu 44–5/ Ussama Azam 02.

Every effort has been made to acknowledge correctly and contact the source/ copyright holder of the images. Welbeck Publishing Group apologizes for any unintentional errors or omissions which will be corrected in future editions of this book.

Opposite. The Library and Learning Centre, University of Economics, Vienna, 2013.

Published in 2024 by OH! Life

An imprint of Welbeck Non-Fiction Limited, part of Welbeck Publishing Group. Offices in London, 20 Mortimer Street, London W1T 3JW, and Sydney, Level 17, 207 Kent Street, Sydney NSW 2000 Australia.www.welbeckpublishing.com

Text and Design © Welbeck Non-Fiction Limited 2024

Cover: Photograph by Junjie Tam/Unsplash

A CIP catalogue record for this book is available from the British Library.

ISBN 978-1-83861-196-5

Publisher: Lisa Dyer
Copyeditor: Katie Hewett
Design: www.gradedesign.com and James Pople
Production controller: Arlene Lestrade

Printed and bound in China

10 9 8 7 6 5 4 3 2 1